CALL OF THE WILD

The Language of Dogs and Other Canines

Megan Kopp

Cavendish Square

New York

Published in 2017 by Cavendish Square Publishing, LLC
243 5th Avenue, Suite 136, New York, NY 10016

Copyright © 2017 by Cavendish Square Publishing, LLC

First Edition

Website: cavendishsq.com

This publication represents the opinions and views of the author based on his or her personal experience, knowledge, and research. The information in this book serves as a general guide only. The author and publisher have used their best efforts in preparing this book and disclaim liability rising directly or indirectly from the use and application of this book.

CPSIA Compliance Information: Batch #CS16CSQ

All websites were available and accurate when this book was sent to press.

Library of Congress Cataloging-in-Publication Data

Names: Kopp, Megan, author.
Title: The language of dogs and other canines / Megan Kopp.
Description: New York : Cavendish Square Publishing, [2016] | Series: Call of the wild | Includes bibliographical references and index.
Identifiers: LCCN 2016005308 (print) | LCCN 2016018530 (ebook) |
ISBN 9781502617347 (pbk.) | ISBN 9781502617255 (library bound) |
ISBN 9781502617132 (6 pack) | ISBN 9781502617194 (ebook)
Subjects: LCSH: Canidae--Behavior--Juvenile literature. |
Dogs--Behavior--Juvenile literature. | Animal communication--Juvenile literature.
Classification: LCC QL737.C22 K78 2016 (print) | LCC QL737.C22 (ebook) |
DDC 599.77159--dc23
LC record available at https://lccn.loc.gov/2016005308

Editorial Director: David McNamara
Editor: Kelly Spence
Copy Editor: Rebecca Rohan
Art Director: Jeffrey Talbot
Designer: Joseph Macri
Production Assistant: Karol Szymczuk
Photo Research: J8 Media

Printed in the United States of America

CONTENTS

Animal Communication

When dogs and other **canines** howl, sniff, or wag their tails, they are not just being dogs. They are communicating. Communication is how animals share information between individuals and groups.

One animal sends a message or a **signal**. A second animal receives the message. The receiver decides what to do with the information. The three main purposes of animal communication are for identification, sharing a location, and influencing behavior.

One way dogs greet one another is by touching noses. This is their way of saying, "Hello."

TALKING WITHOUT WORDS

We communicate with our friends and family by talking. Dogs and other canines can't talk. They send messages in other ways. Some messages are sent by sight. These messages can be passed on without using a lot of energy. They can also be sent while on the move. This is important for wild canines such as wolves, jackals, and foxes.

The problem with visual messages is that they don't work after dark. Sound messages work day or night. They travel quickly and over long distances. **Scent marking** is another effective way to leave a message. Scents stick around long after the sender has left the area, leaving behind its message.

THE SCIENCE BEHIND SCENT MARKING

All canines scent-mark, even **domestic** dogs. Canines mark to let other animals know they are around. They also mark to claim resources, like food and **territory**. **Urine** is a common marker. It contains chemical messages. These messages can include information about a canine's age and whether they are male or female. They also hold clues about an individual's health and whether or not they are a possible mate.

Bloodhounds have an incredible sense of smell. Some of these animals have tracked a single scent for over 130 miles (209 kilometers).

All play and a little talk for these pups!

CHAPTER ONE

The Dish on Dogs

Dogs come in all shapes and sizes. These furry companions use sight, sound, scents, and body language to share information.

READ MY LIP CURL

Dogs often use body language to communicate with each other. A raised lip showing teeth is a warning sign to back off. A direct stare is a sign of **dominance**. If a dog's ears are laid flat against its head, it is a sign of **submission**. A fast, wagging tail shows excitement. When a dog stretches its

When a snarling dog shows its teeth, it is sending a clear message to stay away.

front legs out and lowers its body, it is a sign that it wants to play. This move is called a play bow.

BARK, GROWL, AND HOWL

Dogs howl when they are alone, as a way of looking for company, just like their wolf ancestors. Most dogs bark when they fight, play, or are excited. Sometimes they bark as a warning or to attract attention. Dogs tend to whine when they are sad or lonely, or when they feel afraid or excited. Puppies whimper to show fear or for attention.

SMELLS LIKE MINE

Domestic dogs still share many behaviors with their wild relatives. Both defend their territories and mark them by urinating on trees, rocks, fence posts, and other sites. These **scent posts** tell other dogs that a territory is occupied.

A domestic dog marks its territory throughout the neighborhood.

SPECIES STATS

There are many **breeds**, or kinds, of dogs. Chihuahuas stand about 5 inches (13 centimeters) high at the shoulder and weigh less than 6 pounds (3 kilograms). Irish wolfhounds tower 32 inches (81 cm) high at the shoulder. Saint Bernards weigh up to 170 pounds (77 kg). Dogs are found anywhere humans live in the world. A group of dogs is called a pack.

A hungry pup will lick its mother's muzzle to ask for food. To feed her young, a mother wolf brings up food she has already chewed from her stomach.

CHAPTER TWO

Getting to Know Gray Wolves

Wolves are pack animals. They hunt together, raise their young together, and protect a shared territory. Communication is important for the pack's survival.

HOWL AWAY

Wolves are vocal animals. Sounds, such as howls, allow pack members to communicate with each other about where they are and when it is time to hunt. Howls also let other packs know that a territory is occupied.

Wolves are known for their spine-tingling howls. Howls can send many different messages. A lone wolf howls to attract the attention of its pack. **Communal**, or group, howls may send territorial messages from one pack to another. Some howls are confrontational. Much like barking domestic dogs, wolves may simply begin howling because a nearby wolf is howling already. Wolves also whimper, whine, growl, bark, yelp, and snarl.

SPECIES STATS

Gray wolves live and hunt in groups called packs. These large canines range in weight from 40 to 175 pounds (18 to 79 kg) and stretch up to 63 inches (160 cm) in length. Gray wolves once roamed throughout North America, into Mexico, and across Western Europe. Now they are only found in remote parts of North America.

The top wolf shows its dominance with a snarl. The lower-ranking wolf shows submission by licking the other wolf's mouth.

TOP WOLF

Wolves use facial expressions, scent, body language, and sound to communicate with each other. **Rank**, or which wolf is in charge, is communicated among pack members through body language and facial expressions. Wolves show submission by crouching, touching chins, and rolling over to show their tummies. Scent marking is usually only done by the top male. It is used to communicate with other packs.

A male and female jackal will stay bonded as mates for many years.

CHAPTER THREE

Calling All Jackals

L ike wolves, jackals are vocal animals. Unlike wolves, jackals do not form large packs. But they do work together to find food by using vocal signals.

Jackals hunt during the cool, night hours. They can hunt down their own food, but they are just as happy to eat animals that have been killed by another **predator**. A jackal will howl when an animal like a lion makes a kill. This brings other jackals to the area. These jackals are members of an extended family who share a territory. When a lion leaves the leftovers, the jackals dive in.

A pair of black-headed jackals feast on a carcass.

The average jackal litter has between one and nine pups. Adult jackals use rumbling growls and special barks to warn their young to hide when there is danger nearby.

THE SCIENCE BEHIND HOWLING

Howls are used to find each other. Each family has a slightly different call than the next. This helps keep groups spaced out across an area. It reduces the need to compete for food sources.

Different species of jackals use slightly different calls for communication. Scientists believe that males and females will also howl together in a chorus. This call is a type of **bonding** activity.

SPECIES STATS

There are three main species of jackals. They are found in Africa, southeastern Europe, and southern Asia. Jackals live alone, in pairs, or in small family groups called packs. Adult jackals weight 15 to 24 pounds (7 to 11 kg). They are most active at dusk. They eat small animals and plants.

An individual jackal, known as a "helper," might stay with its parents for one or two years to help raise the next litter.

Red foxes are quieter than their more vocal wolf and jackal cousins.

CHAPTER FOUR

Red Foxes' Messages

Wolves howl. Dogs bark. Jackals yell, yap, growl, and howl. What about red foxes? How do they communicate?

QUIET AS A FOX

Foxes are normally silent animals, but that doesn't mean they never make sounds. Young foxes bark for their mother's attention. Adults send out warning calls and make noises to find mates.

MAKING SCENTS

Foxes are **solitary** in nature. Leaving scent messages is a good way to communicate over long distances. Foxes use urine to mark their home **range** and pass on other information. This is called scent marking. Foxes make scent stations at set spots. This tells other foxes in the area who is nearby.

A keen sense of smell and excellent sense of hearing are important for the red fox. A fox can hear a tiny mouse squeak from about 100 feet (30 m) away.

Scientists have discovered that scent marking has many different purposes. Researchers found that foxes urinate on leftover food such as bones, bird wings, and dried pieces of skin. This stinky scent sends the message that no

A mother fox keeps a close eye on her active young, which are called kits.

food is present, or it is not worth checking out. Foxes are **scavengers** and eat almost anything. They regularly patrol their territory hunting for food. Scent marking helps them find more food in a shorter period of time.

SPECIES STATS

Red foxes live in many different parts of the world. They can be found from the Arctic Circle to North Africa, from Central America to northern Asia. Red foxes do not form packs. When the pups are young, they make up a small family unit with their moms. Adult foxes weigh up to 24 pounds (11 kg).

Chaser is one bright border collie! Over three years, Chaser's owner spent four to five hours a day teaching his pet to identify different toys, including balls, Frisbees, and stuffed animals.

CHAPTER FIVE

Dog Talk

Dogs can understand if we are happy or sad or mad just by looking at our faces. They show affection by nuzzling or licking when their owners are upset. They can even understand many human words. On average, dogs are able to understand around 150 words. Come. Stay. Down. Play. Hungry. Ball. One smart border collie named Chaser can understand over 1,000 words.

Dr. Brian Hare is an associate professor at Duke University in North Carolina. He studies canine

intelligence. He's excited that dogs like Chaser are able to learn labels for objects just like humans do. Hare hopes to unlock how dogs think and learn and pass this knowledge on to dog trainers. This information could make it faster and easier to train working dogs and companion animals that help children with **autism** and people with disabilities.

Seeing-eye dogs are one type of canine companion. These dogs are specially trained to guide visually impaired people around objects.

Hare has created a web-based app called Dognition. It allows people to test their own dog's smarts and record the results online. Researchers then use this information to further their understanding of canine intelligence.

IN THE FIELD

Dave Roberts is a computer science professor at North Carolina State University. He and his team are inventing new ways to talk and listen to dogs. They are using technology to help understand what dogs are saying to humans and vice versa. Roberts uses a special harness that allows researchers to send wireless commands to dogs in the form of **vibrations**. Sensors on the harness send information from the dog back to researchers.

Glossary

autism A disorder which makes it difficult for some people to communicate and interact with others.

bonding Forming a close relationship.

breeds Kinds of animals within a species with distinct features.

canines Members of the dog family with distinctive pointed, canine teeth.

communal Shared by a group.

domestic Describing an animal that has been tamed and trained by humans.

dominance The power and influence of one individual over another.

intelligence The ability to understand and learn.

predator An animal that hunts and kills its food.

range The space where an animal lives.

rank Position.

scavengers Animals that feed on dead animals and food scraps.

scent marking Leaving a scent behind, usually as urine or feces, that communicates a message.

scent posts Items marked by an animal's scent.

signal A sound or action used to send a message or warning.

solitary Being by oneself.

submission The action of giving in to a stronger individual.

territory An area belonging to one individual or group.

urine A liquid waste material often referred to as pee.

vibrations Movements that can be felt.

Find Out More

Books

Gagne, Tammy. *Speaking Dog: Understanding Why Your Hound Howls and Other Tips on Speaking Dog*. Dog Ownership. Mankato, MN: Capstone Press, 2012.

Newman, Aline Alexander, and Gary Weitzman. *How to Speak Dog: A Guide to Decoding Dog Language*. Washington, DC: National Geographic Children's Books, 2013.

Websites

BBC Nature Wildlife: Dogs

www.bbc.co.uk/nature/life/Canidae

Learn about different members of the canine family.

National Geographic Kids: Gray Wolf

kids.nationalgeographic.com/animals/gray-wolf/#gray-wolf-closeup.jpg

Learn all about gray wolves.

Index

About the Author

Megan Kopp is a freelance writer whose passions include science, nature, and the outdoors. She is the author of close to sixty titles for young readers. She loves research and has even gone so far as volunteering to be rescued from a snow cave to get a story about training avalanche rescue dogs. Kopp lives in the foothills of the Canadian Rocky Mountains, where she spends her spare time hiking, camping, and canoeing with her border collie, Taylor.